# Painted Women in the Walls

*poems by*

# Jenny Benjamin

*Finishing Line Press*
Georgetown, Kentucky

# Painted Women
# in the Walls

## ACKNOWLEDGMENTS

"Bat Love,"—Art + Literature Lab online series: "How to Live"
"Magician," "Empress I," and "Sylvia's Hives," "Why Abide?," and "Closer to
Sundown" —WUWM Lake Effect Radio Program and Website
"Clutched by a Nearly Noon Sun"—*The Diagram*
"Beauty"—*Fox Cry Review*

Publisher: Leah Huete de Maines
Editor: Christen Kincaid
Cover Art: Drawing by Adam Ithier, @adamithierart,
          Watercolor by Ali Benjamin
Author Photo: Philip D. Stockton
Cover Design: Elizabeth Maines McCleavy

Order online: www.finishinglinepress.com
        also available on amazon.com

Author inquiries and mail orders:
Finishing Line Press
PO Box 1626
Georgetown, Kentucky 40324
USA

# Contents

Magician ............................................................................. 1

Empress I ........................................................................... 2

Empress II .......................................................................... 3

Clutched by a Nearly Noon Sun ...................................... 4

Sylvia's Hives .................................................................. 12

Beauta Beatrix ................................................................ 13

Moses .............................................................................. 14

Beauty ............................................................................. 15

Names Will Never ......................................................... 16

Why Abide? .................................................................... 18

April Love ....................................................................... 20

Bat Love .......................................................................... 21

The Golden Fairy and the White Bear .......................... 22

Closer to Sundown ........................................................ 25

*For Adam, Ali, Maggie, and Sophia*
*the love you bring*

## Magician

I can divine these brambles,
or the gnarled flowers at my feet.
They obscure my heels as I
float on yellow horizons,
tip the diagonal of my arms into
the numbers of years set down like dust.
I can, you see, lead you somewhere,
over rock and highland green.
I can conjure stone from earth
to make a window to another world.
Come with me. Take the tips of my fingers.
Interlace the leaves and set down
your sword, your wand.
You have no need for all the people
who make up your mind.
You have no need for the lily or rose
jabbing between your legs like a crude
lover. Walk this way with me,
and I will tip the stars down your throat.
Drop the grapes and roll them over the skin
of your neck. Only then will you have
the idea of splendor. Of the eternal.
All you need is this staff to guide your way.
All you need is to follow the shift
of my eyes. I may lead you somewhere,
or you could go the other way.
Sit down at my table. I'll flip forever
like a figure eight. I'll let you look
at me for as long as it takes.
Let's begin. I promise. This is something
you won't forget.

## Empress I

The wind has stopped.
No jeweled throne in nature's
yellow pall of sky, and I have
seen the river moving from me
like a lover I have not kissed yet,
who does not know I am here, reclined,
waiting for the cut-down rye to stop
blowing in the cloudless sky.

I have not found the wreath for my grave,
nor my way into the dark of pine forest
behind me. It calls me like the feral cries
of animals mating. I cannot turn my eyes.

I have searched for one open sound to surface
amid the quiet of my days, but not one visits me.
And I am left in the stillness of the air,
hoping something will make him turn back,
that he will come my way.

It only takes one.

**Empress II**

Translucent river of salt and stones.
It runs to the sea in the middle of marshy islands
with dolphins humped above the water like bobbing
children learning to swim.

He builds boats to put upon the river.
I tend the slope of my thighs.

## Clutched by a Nearly Noon Sun

### I. Husband & Wife

"Il colonnato," he said
     Eva's face over and over again
     like falling pennies or onions tearing apart.
The colonnade,
     suicidally beautiful, as aerated roots are lazing up and down.
He is burdened by this fury of offices and ceremonies, sulky
organisms.

She flinches. "Hazardous," he says, to be the bedridden husband,
     and she is closer to Rome than to him, really,
     interludes of countryside, lipstick, cabbage-roses
make him incendiary
     hiz-za hiz-za wife and lover
burned down like isolated trees in an uproar off the tin roof in one
shining-shot.

He witnessed it all:
     the man's mouth, tongue (that palmy son-of-a-bitch)
     on her eyelid, legs over and over again
his private convalescence of dying.
     *Where's the baby?*
Pray among the rocks, green stone, and beet fields,

the dragged furls of satin ribbons
     sheets from piano lessons
     in a crate
*Where's the baby, pray?*
     Between beet fields and green stone in a graveyard
Her own baby: ghost plume among falling pennies, onions

tearing apart.

## II. Boy & Mother

The boy knows the history of
        kick-can in
        Florida summer,
hanging on the farm fence smashing coins on the tracks
        playing his little box, smokin' rocks
string music hollow at the wrist.

He tired of his mother's
        hush-baby talk and glass of whiskey,
        her carved strangers in the bed.
He wants to break the net and swim
        the black earth back to fresh grasses
and the asses of the girls

the pleats in her dress, her small elbow bones
        drive him huzza-huzza,
        make him slap the live oak of his hollow
fire each night the drip of light blue tears
        from his scanty fanning, his groan
and palm-wine baptism.

All because of her unpinned hair,
        her under the hedge sensations,
        pale and domestic, but he's afraid
to quench his quiet purple of the river bottom.
        Instead he makes
his mama's supper: boiled potatoes and

dark bread.

III. Stranger & Woman

A saffron-robed stranger shared a cab with her,
    and they got down to it:
        temporized six hawks between them
a buckling warmth almost visible,
        the air drunk to the limits of the earth.
The man's face had an oddness to it,

but when open-mouthed, she was a landscape,
    a nacreous gleam
    in a ticking moment
discord, pipe and crude drum
    sounds broke the downhill
of their limbs; he raked them with his long field

of olive trees; his eyes saw various arrangements
    of curves and angles,
        silky breast, the drinkest deep
yoked to his middle, up him to a fantasy of praxis.
    Two bottles of wine and an aspirin

are all he had since last night.

Time to maze out of this haze
    to her lusty
    lace and collarbones
in a blast of cab-ride
    mingled with suffering Jeremiahs,
a moat of red wine, these hawks,

huge windows.

IV. Mother & Husband

Her mood ground corn, raked the sockets
    of the hull till raw.
    She shed the fish scales like birds
breaking wings over yellow seas.
    This pocket of white belly hollow.
This vanished nursery.

These small cages the days become.
    Her stomach iron and deafened lead.
    The lambs have broken, the fury gone,
a mountain pressed down to stone.
    She wishes for bitter pith;
instead, he lives, jabbering shadow in

dirty fingernails.

V. Woman & Son

"Mama got you," he, just shy of two, used to say when scared
        from the stirring wind of his curtains.
    The smoke-tinged breeze, her cigarette
and bruised thigh in the room with broken sunlight,
        dust, and a murky ringing from the TV.
Sand and oil spots she sees

now, clumsy and shapeless figures,
        but how she gave birth to a fine boy
        years ago living near the river in Georgia,
the mystery of the muddy river bottom, poplar trees,
        and willows.
"The boy gonna be a hood like his daddy."
She needs a longitude of hours, boiling hot
        Ethiopian kings, or children leaving
        a dance. Rum punch and pineapple drinks
her medicines. There's the boy now, all nose drip and splendor,
        clanking pans. He puts the potatoes in a shining
blue bowl. They sit and the wind

stirs them.

## VI. Man & Wife

"Unreal Ahab," he says to himself, out due east of the city,
      out for some revenge on something,
      probably his wife, for existing, for living in sickness.
He leaves the woman not his wife and must wash himself
      with a cloth, must exorcize the buzz of mid-morning
in Whitechapel. He pulls his robes to himself, an overcoat

of cold grace, easily opened and closed again to his wilderness.
      He arrives home to his immaculate stillness
      and divested charms, only a tomb of cleansed lemon
where he'll wash his wife, feed her medicines,
      roll her to the bed.
He'll write a letter to his father:

he'll understand his son's charcoal underbelly,
      brown and gray sketches to each day,
      and the instance of vibrancy in one cab-ride
gone now with only his goddamned buzz left.
      He hears his wife call his name;
each time he cannot help but catch

his breath.

VII. Traveler & Man

Mid-morning in Whitechapel. She's fresh back from the continent,
        that glossy spray holiday; her backpack like the marble steps
of Italy.
        She'd stripped down in her dorm room and showered in the
rusted room
in flip flops bought at Camden. "Top ten showers," she thought, "of
all time,"
        took her time with lotion and decided on a v-neck blouse
with gold lace,
an extravagance, music in the old hinges her worn legs became on
the cobblestones

of Prague, German hostels, the dark bread mornings and thick
coffee, jam like petals
        in the mouth, the women washing lower panes of windows
in Vienna;
        she's closer to Rome than to anywhere else: the dark pews of
white churches,
cold hammer traffic, the sky wild with ruins and smog. Her only
task: to scrutinize
        the afternoon through eyelashes wet with water from
fountains, to juggle
words and phrases: un museo, dove il bagno? Un papagallo verde.
Savory,
sputtering eggs inside her mouth; her mind ping-ponged grammar
and verb tenses,
        hordes of unpinned sensations, a dank woodland nel un
soprabito,
        the overcoat, Tolstoy? No, Gogol? Panting bonfires in
catacombs
of stolen monasteries. Now she rides the east-end rickety tube with
nostalgia
        for her second home, America a fat balloon of amusements
drifting

farther away. At Whitechapel the crowds wail mundane movements
from stoplight to crosswalk, and as she turns away from the station, a
robed man stands near a waiting car. His eyes, black wells for hiding
places, thickening
        embers with climates arid and expansive. His squint at the
nearly noon sun
and this slight bird tread glance at her makes her sink, a sprouting
downward into cement,
        a clutching wind moves her. Somehow, she takes this as a
signal
and shares a cab with him, though she has little money.

The pounds in the palm of his hand. The possible slide
        of his crimson robe.
        His dark skin.
His loose curls of brown hair, a cloakroom for her hands.
        His patient face.
She sees while wandering the lilied pools

at Kew.

## Sylvia's Hives

The husband is a frozen wing of a bird,
flesh and feather yarned to bone.
They are bones, painted rooms, and shallow
pools bodies make when they exhaust everything.

The wife manages the shepherd's pie, jarred honey
extracted from her own swarming hives, where her
bees stung him one time in the face as she curled
herself on the bed nursing her newborn son.

The minutes are honey drips from the cedar closet's
spoon, wet wood from a toddler's licks. The zoo visit
just in time for the lion's blood feeding on white rabbits,
and she cannot curry once more the throbbing

thunder pains of him as he found the skin and fur
of another woman so sleek and warm, too warm to resist.
She can see how he'd burrow beneath the woman's wet heat.
She can see his heaving chest catching its breath.

She craves to taste dirt, feels the drenched wool pull
of her womb with whispering life, but in the end she
hates typing his pages, his burnt-colored neck,
his words and more words barking from three heads.

She dies with a towel wrapped tightly, vapors and mist,
eyelashes over ether. The cool laundry list folded away.
Pink sheets of paper. Babies sleeping, heavy as their names.

## Beauta Beatrix
*For Lizzie Siddel*

Charcoal on hands, he sketches me; my prints fall away
From the grace of my days motionless in water,
Or sitting for him. I am on Laura's pedestal carved
By Petrarch with his sonnets. These men are so far off
From me: the poets, painters, shades of Italy in the distance.

*Reframe the will of painted women in the walls.*

No more London's dark damp lit by lamps and heated
Water for Ophelia's heart. I have a tincture to soothe anguish
As each day this woman I am brings. It will repair in drops
And let down the hair of the hours I spend still until I am
A better lover, one who doesn't want to marry but will open
Her legs a little for them to touch with one brush stroke.

*Reframe the will of painted women in the walls.*

I have decided I will not come again. Some do.
Those Greeks dipped again and again until the horizon
Of all their lives blurred with asphodel and the memory
Of clay pots filled with spices from other lands.
I have not lived yet, except that one time the possibility
Of a life away from millinery. I walked alone in the east end
With my mind a wrap of soot left from candle flame
For I had an idea, hot and careless, to be a painter and a poet.
Instead, I became the statue with a shadow cast by the hand
Of a man.

*Reframe the will of painted women in the walls.*

I have an underside. This mystery illuminates my measures
Of divine parts. My dirty parts. My parts that never made it
Beyond oils of the English countryside. Here's the tincture
Drip again to sink beneath the only rock that hides mercy.

*Reframe the will of painted women in the walls.*

**Moses**

Triptych of a mother, daughter, and infant son reaching
a doughy hand to his mother's cheek.
The daughter looks at him on tip toes with a crude basket
beneath her arm, the one to set it all in motion.

The mother, brown skin, thick black waves of hair like charcoal-
colored wire teased back, a prominent nose making a line of sorrow
from her eyes to the face of her son.

The marsh behind them opens to a green-black river,
so the basket and their small world is sent away.

Into a splatter of waves, the basket bobs duck-like
on the water's lips, then stops in a tangled gathering
of brittle reeds.

Hollow screaming slices air, but no one hears the babe,
for the woman and the girl are far away because the river
sets a course unknown, one that takes away.

The river swallows all the wails and rocks the baby boy.
He cries until he can cry no more.
And so the story ended there.

## Beauty

For once she felt beautiful:
the hat her daughter bought her.
She called it an extravagance,
but secretly she took it to her
creaky bed with ironed sheets
and set the box down so carefully,
silently shutting the door so that no one
would hear the slight opening of the box
or the crinkle of tissue paper.
She put the velvety blues, dark greens,
and maroons on top of her head gently.
She slowly led her new head,
dressed like a Christmas tree
stacked with ornaments to the angel,
to the mirror.

My grandmother felt beautiful,
for a moment, until she heard the heavy
feet of young men in the hall,
prowling for their supper.

## Names Will Never

I have been called whorecuntbitchslut
by more than one man, and what I
sometimes pictured when I heard those
words was my dad, after he was changed
by stroke, and how these words would
have been gibberish, but somehow he
would understand. His large, round eyes,
fallen-leaf brown, would pool with tears,
and his lips, always breaking into a wide
turn-the-tables on a bad conversation smile,
would quiver with hurt because these men
called me names that impale the heart.

*Names will never*

I have been called selfishcuntworthlesswhore
by more than one man, and what I
sometimes pictured when I heard those
words were my children, how those words
would make them breathe fire
that burns through a green valley.

*Names will never*

I have been called stupidbitchshamelessslut
by more than one man, and what I
sometimes pictured when I heard those
words was myself, as a little girl, how I
spent hours making up stories in my head
while tucked inside our lilac bush or
wandering to the needle bed beneath
pines, but never had I ever thought up
those words. My lips wobbled on words
like *Lochness, Sasquatch, Shenandoah,
unicorn, mystery, wonder, kittens.*
No stupid bitch. No selfish cunt.

Names will never break me, yet
how do I extinguish memory?

## Why Abide?

As a child I was the one on the muck-brown lakeshore,
calling for my big sister to come in, *please*,
making sure I'd see her sleek hair and wide eyes
pop above the surface, and each time my breath
would catch. So easily she dove and sprang,
her feet puncturing air and disappearing
like mermaid fins.

I, the landlocked mermaid burying my thighs
in pebbly sand, waited for my sister to split
the water with her shore-bound legs, finally finished,
another breath released, and she'd lead me back
to the worn-out sheet, filled with sand, and
the beach towels, damp, yet welcoming, then
silently, we'd make our way back. She the only
one of us with the fatigue of muscles and tendons,
from hours under water.

I trailed her and watched how her feet turned slightly
outward when she walked, the dents deeper on the
sides when she marched through sand, and I thought
this was caused by mermaid fins that morphed
back to feet for land, and we wouldn't talk about
anything, just felt the twilight come in purple swaths
across a sky invaded by darkening treetops,
where hills met the horizon with a kiss.

Can you imagine a world where the mermaids
are told they cannot swim, and if they do, they may
be grappled with and told anything the mermen want
to say, they cannot speak up or are made to stuff
their mermaid mouths with water weeds and silt
until they look like dolls, hollow eyes and empty
hands?

Can you imagine these sisters having to tell each other
anything else than you can swim all day if you want
or just watch your toes seep beneath the soaked sand,
let the lake water lap at your ankles and know
you are magnificent. You are supposed to be here.

Let's lead our sisters to the shores and step in,
and take the water with us as we swim.

## April Love

The summer will not tame us,
For we have found the ivy secret
With roots throbbing beneath us.
We part the purple need of my
Veins run blue away from a heart
Stopped still, my hand clutches
A whispery veil as I turn away
From the sun.

April love has run the length of me
As I saw him first at the train.
April love left me torn between
The native plants that blanket
The fields back home and the potted
Lilies in a garden with golden buildings
And bricked walks. For in those places
I became a woman who could love.
But love deforms and chisels our selves
Into marble folds, making shadows
And ripples of lives entwined,
Abundance with the choice.

But no choice was made because my loves
Of an April in the past stopped underneath
A bridge. Then each lover went the other way,
And I left youth behind. Years later I became
A mother, cloaked figure through an opening gate.

## Bat Love

Cradled in the instinct of not just yet
you are here and I am holding on like a hoary bat
with frost-tinged fur and worry claws clinging
taut with need and frenzied yes I can hold on forever
you under me as we dangle from a tree branch with earth
steady below these three babies beneath with easy turn
of mouth to teat to drink from my dissolving self of years
ago how well-rested I looked in photographs and daisy
like open-faced to the days without the little ones stitched
to me on the underside weary and afraid I might slip up
and ruin you but here my hands run with sinew to wings
so then I may not fly but it's a trajectory of maybe I can
hold on until the universe makes its way to one point
for a little while more the cells of my membranes and yours
will hold out for this blink of time we call life

# The Golden Fairy and the White Bear

I.

*Everything I seem to write is a love story.*

Tallow drop and hyacinth kingdoms of precious gems
blooming in the heart all because they have fallen in love:
the fairy of the desert, caramel brown and glistening, living on a small
green patch
beneath the trunk of an orange tree, holding her basket of cake.
And he: the great white bear,
man of delights with lions roaring from his chest,
thick mangles of hair, girth and magnitude vast,
but his eyes are calm whispers, his touch feathers from a dove.

Rain drops
        Winds blow
The right curve in the neighborhood of heart.

In the midst of moon rays, they meet,
                unlikely, each stuffing down feelings of half-rotten
timbers, past disappointments,
        belts of rare sorrow.

He's furry, she shadow and bronze.
She offers him cake, sugar candy on his tongue.
There is a salutary freshness in the air, a tendency to promise.
Around them a little ring of moon lace: they inhabit this island, a place
of remarkable warmth, despite the night, fierce rays, golden light
surround them all because they have met each other.
They lay on pillows of silk and kiss, bundle red as blood together,
hearts like open sea, spirits on Mediterranean shores.
*This day is favorable*, he thinks: yellow caress, basket of cake.

At times the logistics of their love is tricky:
        His claws ravage her delicate wings.
"They'll grow back," she says, but she knows the process is painful
pinpricks

shooting from her back.

He sighs, hangs his head in the curve of a bow; he gnaws the claw tips.

II.

Troubles happen.

The Golden Fairy's fragile toes ache.

The great White Bear sweats cloud puffs in the desert.

Naysayers croon and chatter about their differences, say how she or he

should go back to where each came from, and yet, she sprouted from the

rolling sands, and he broke through and lumbered down the mountain.

Both are of the earth, and together a canvas tent protects them, a tent home.

Home. Tent. Something to build and collapse when needed.

III.

Illuminated terror, they must escape and venture into the trees.

She cannot fly yet, because her wings grow again, breaking through shoulder blades with a

Crack, crack that makes him wince. So he carries her over his massive back,

in the overwhelming humidity, the sands churning in abundant clouds.

"Heaven bless you," she says into his furry ear, and he shudders from her voice, thick like muddy reeds in swamp water.

He keeps it light, "Is heaven made of winter? If so, then I want to go there."

She giggles, and his heart explodes.

But the torches follow them in bobbing blazes.

"Little more," he says and moves closer to the mountain.

Both know their bodies as specimens will fetch a good price. And the unusual of their pairing
makes some hate and call them something for the shoe-soles.

The fairy shows the hurt in her sighs, the bear in his roars over morning milk.

Summer thunderstorms, he wants a bridge north, no more discomfort, just high air, daytime winds, a thicket to slumber in with the fairy folded beneath him.

IV.
*Everything I seem to write is a love story,*
the narrator says again, and the listeners sit on cushions, ears open meadows.
*How does it end?*
*What do you think?*
The fairy now wears feathers of gold; they live under the mountain ash and sleep on beds of poplar leaves; they eat chestnuts and drink from magic fountains.
*Yes, that is so.*

## Closer to Sundown

Are those willo-the-wisps to lead me along a new path?
Or has the water tricked my eyes to believe in myth?
These feathers, really leaves making golden pillow puddles,
take shape, and will they fade with sunset at the close of day?

I see my mother's patient face teaching me to roll dough,
get out a stain, swing a station wagon on a dime turn.
Then two-by-two my older daughters walk, my youngest
trailing in a band of light spanning water and a seam
of endless green.

My fingers touch their shadows on the ground.
I look and see all there is to see: children living
in a theory of vines climbing red brick
not knowing where the twists will lead,
and I want to hold them

here

like this

in my hand

but they go like words meeting the universe and disappearing.

Instead of stricken to a stop, I proceed, as if my tendons, sinew,
and muscles are not collapsing, a report to the ever-changing.
My bones, I wear around my neck to mark the transformation.
I am a selkie shedding waxy skin into pools of coming midnight.

Children, let me enter your shadows on the spring green.
I will teach you how to feel the orange glow of falling sun
and the hours sung from cardinal song.
I've found this is the perfect world for growing older
or growing up: miniature landscapes of cascading gold
and silver dawns, where here we move through folds
of light.

**Jenny Benjamin** is the owner of her freelance writing and editing business JB Communications, LLC. Over fifty of her poems have appeared in journals, including *DIAGRAM, South Carolina Review, Fulcrum, Baltimore Review, Chelsea,* and the *Crab Orchard Review.* Her first novel, *This Most Amazing,* was published in 2013 by Armida Books in Nicosia, Cyprus. Her poetry chapbook, *More Than a Box of Crayons,* was published by Finishing Line Press in February 2018. Her poetry chapbook, *Midway,* earned second place in the 2017 No Chair Press contest and was published in April 2018. *Enhanced* and *Corrupted,* the first two books of her young adult, science fiction trilogy were published by Ananke Press (October 2021, July 2022). *Redeemed: Book Three of the Terrian Trilogy* came out in January 2023. Her novel *Heather Finch* was published by Running Wild Press (June 2022). She lives in Milwaukee, Wisconsin.